Spaghetti and Meatballs for All! A Mathematical Story

Spaghetti and Meatballs for All! A Mathematical Story

written by Marilyn Burns

illustrated by Debbie Tilley

A Marilyn Burns Brainy Day Book

SCHOLASTIC INC.

New York Toronto London Auckland Sydney
Mexico City New Delhi Hong Kong Buenos Aires

This book was originally published in hardcover by Scholastic Press in 1997.

ISBN-13: 978-0-545-04445-5
ISBN-10: 0-545-04445-6

12 11 10 9 8 7 6 5 4   9 10 11 12 13/0

Printed in the U.S.A. 40
First Bookshelf edition, August 2008

Design and art direction by Aileen Friedman

For Evan.—D.T.

One fine day, Mrs. Comfort was busy tending the lettuce patch in her garden.

"You know, it's been a long time since we've seen the family," she said to her husband.

"You're right," answered Mr. Comfort. He was stretched out on a bench doing what he liked to do best in a vegetable garden—reading a cookbook.

"Maybe it's time for a family reunion," Mrs. Comfort said.

"A wonderful idea," Mr. Comfort agreed. "Hmm, let's see. Menus, menus. Dinner for two. Serves four to six. Banquets. How many people would we be having?" he asked.

The Comforts called their children. They called their parents. Mrs. Comfort called her brother. Mr. Comfort called the next-door neighbors, who were almost like family. Everyone could come.

"That's 32 people altogether, including us," Mr. Comfort said. "What could possibly fit in our oven and still feed 32 people?" he wondered out loud.

"Why not make your famous spaghetti and meatballs?" asked Mrs. Comfort.

"Good thinking," said Mr. Comfort.

"Now, what about renting some tables and chairs?" asked Mrs. Comfort. She got out thc tclcphonc book.

Two weeks later, the big day arrived.

Mr. Comfort got up very early and spent all morning cooking. He baked 16 loaves of garlic bread and made eight pounds of fresh pasta. He simmered eight quarts of spaghetti sauce and rolled 96 meatballs.

Mrs. Comfort picked all her ripe tomatoes, cucumbers, and lettuce for salad.

While Mrs. Comfort waited for the tables and chairs she had rented, she drew a seating plan. Then she got out the dishes, the silverware, the glasses, the tablecloths, and some vases.

But when the rental company arrived, they were one chair short.

"Don't worry," said Mr. Comfort. "You'll think of something."

Mrs. Comfort found a folding chair. Now the tables were ready. Each had four place settings, four chairs, and a vase with lovely cut flowers. Mr. Comfort came out of the kitchen balancing eight plates of celery and olives, one for each table.

Just after noon, the Comforts' daughter and her husband arrived with their two children.

"Welcome," said Mrs. Comfort.

"Come, sit," said Mr. Comfort.

"Let's push two tables together so you can sit with us," suggested the Comforts' daughter.

"But there won't be room . . ." Mrs. Comfort said.

"But there is," said Mr. Comfort. "There's plenty of room *and* plenty of garlic bread."

Everyone was just about to sit down when a car pulled into the driveway. Mrs. Comfort's brother and his wife, their daughter, her husband, and their twin sons all spilled out.

"Welcome," said Mr. Comfort. "Sit down, sit down."

"Oh, let's push over two more tables so we can all sit together," said Mrs. Comfort's brother's wife. The Comforts' daughter and her husband got up to help.

"But that won't work," said Mrs. Comfort.

"You're so right," Mr. Comfort said. "We'll have to push two more tables together."

"But that won't work, either," said Mrs. Comfort.

"You're right," said Mrs. Comfort's brother's wife.

"Make way!" shouted Mrs. Comfort's brother and the Comforts' son-in-law. They each carried over a table and put them side by side. "You don't understand," Mrs. Comfort sighed. "My plan was . . ." But no one heard her. Everyone was too busy.

"Save some of that garlic bread for me!" a new arrival called.

"Me, too!" "Me, too!" "Me, too!" three more voices piped in.

"Well, look who's here," said Mrs. Comfort's brother's daughter's husband. It was the Comforts' next-door neighbors with their daughter and son.

"Hello, hello!" said Mr. Comfort. "So glad to see you. Have a seat while I get more garlic bread."

"But there *is* no place for them to sit," said Mrs. Comfort.

"Don't worry," said Mrs. Comfort's brother's wife. "We'll just divide these tables into two groups of four."

"Go ahead," Mrs. Comfort said, "but I'm telling you, when . . ."

"You fret too much," said Mr. Comfort. "Bread, anyone?"

When all of the tables had been rearranged, everyone sat down.
"See, Mom?" the Comforts' daughter said. "It worked out just fine."
Mrs. Comfort sighed.

"Hi, ya! Hi, ya! Hi, ya!" boomed a familiar voice. Mr. Comfort's father, mother, and their little terrier strolled in.

"Hello, Grandma. Hello, Grandpa," the Comforts' daughter shouted.

"Oh, dear," said Mrs. Comfort. "Where are they going to sit?"

"No problem," said Mr. and Mrs. Comfort's next-door neighbor. "If we just push all eight tables into one long line, there'll be room enough for everyone."

"Actually . . ." Mrs. Comfort began to explain.

"Absolutely," said Mr. Comfort. He was carrying several big bowls of salad. "Better move fast or this salad will be *really* tossed!"

No sooner had everyone gotten settled than Mrs. Comfort's mother and father drove up in their yellow convertible.

"Hello, Grammy! Hello, Gramps!" the Comforts' daughter shouted.

Mrs. Comfort put down her fork.

"Oh, dear," she said.

"Don't worry. We're all family, right?" Gramps said. "Let's just split this long line of tables in two. There will be plenty of room for us to squeeze in."

"But it still isn't going to work because . . ." Mrs. Comfort started to say. A bowl of salad slid into her lap.

"Sorry," said one of Mrs. Comfort's brother's daughter's twin sons.

Mr. and Mrs. Comfort and their 18 relatives and neighbors were finally all seated. They passed the salad and the bread. They shared the celery and the olives. And when they heard a cheery "Hi, everyone!" most of them held on to their plates.

The Comforts' son and his wife pedaled in on a bicycle for two. Their twin daughters rolled in on skates.

"Didn't I tell you?" Mrs. Comfort said. "There's not enough room."

"No problem, Mom," said the Comforts' son. "We'll just divide these two lines of tables into four pairs. Okey-dokey?"

"Wait! Wait! You're all forgetting something," said Mrs. Comfort.

"We're out of salad over here," the Comforts' daughter said.

"Don't put any tomatoes in mine," said the Comforts' next-door neighbor's son.

"Is there more garlic bread?" asked Mrs. Comfort's mother.

"Who's got my silverware?" asked Mr. Comfort's father.

"Hey," Mrs. Comfort's brother's daughter's son said to his twin brother, "that's my bread you're eating!"

"Get your fingers out of my salad!" the Comforts' son's daughter said to her twin sister.

"Don't play with your food," said the Comforts' son's wife.

"What did you say?" asked Mr. Comfort.

"I said . . ." Mrs. Comfort said.

BEEP! BEEP! A big red van parked at the curb. Out jumped Mrs. Comfort's sister with her husband and their triplets. All three of the triplets had brought their boyfriends, who were also triplets.

"*Now* do you see what I mean?" Mrs. Comfort asked. "Where are they all going to sit?"

"Well, my dearest," said Mr. Comfort. "I haven't served the spaghetti yet. We'll just move a few chairs, reset a few places, and there will be plenty of room for everyone."

"I give up!" cried Mrs. Comfort. She sat down in her chair and didn't budge.

"I say we divide the four pairs of tables into eight single tables," Mrs. Comfort's brother said. He and his wife moved one pair of tables apart. The triplets and their boyfriends moved the other three pairs.

"You see?" said Mr. Comfort. "It all worked out."

"I see everything is back exactly the way I had it!" said Mrs. Comfort.

"I knew you'd think of something," said Mr. Comfort. "Now, how many meatballs would you like?"

For Parents, Teachers, and Other Adults

*I*n school, children learn that area is the space a shape's surface covers, usually measured in square units. They learn that perimeter is the distance around a shape, measured in units of length. These concepts are often abstract and confusing for children. *Spaghetti and Meatballs for All!* presents ideas about area and perimeter in a real-world context. The story also helps children recognize that shapes with the same area can have different perimeters.

The mathematical content in this book is presented in a way that will delight children and help develop their love of reading. *Spaghetti and Meatballs for All!* is meant to stimulate children's imaginations, so invite reactions and comments while you're reading together. Some children may interrupt the story to express an idea or ask a question. Some may want to talk about the illustrations. Other children prefer to listen until the end. Encourage children's participation and follow their leads!

About the Mathematics

At the beginning of the story, Mrs. Comfort knew that 32 people would be coming to the family reunion. She correctly figured out that she could seat all of them at eight small square tables, each with four places. (Fig. 1)

Fig. 1

Although Mrs. Comfort didn't use mathematical terms to describe her plan, it's possible to use area and perimeter to talk about her solution. If you think about the top of each small square table as having the area of 1 square unit, then the perimeter of each individual table is 4 units or one 1 unit of length for each side.

When the Comforts' daughter, her husband, and their two children arrived, they pushed two tables together so that the four of them could sit with Mr. and Mrs. Comfort. This arrangement, which made a rectangular table with an area of 2 square units and a perimeter of 6 units, worked for the time being. Only Mrs. Comfort realized that there wouldn't be enough places when the rest of the guests came. (Fig. 2)

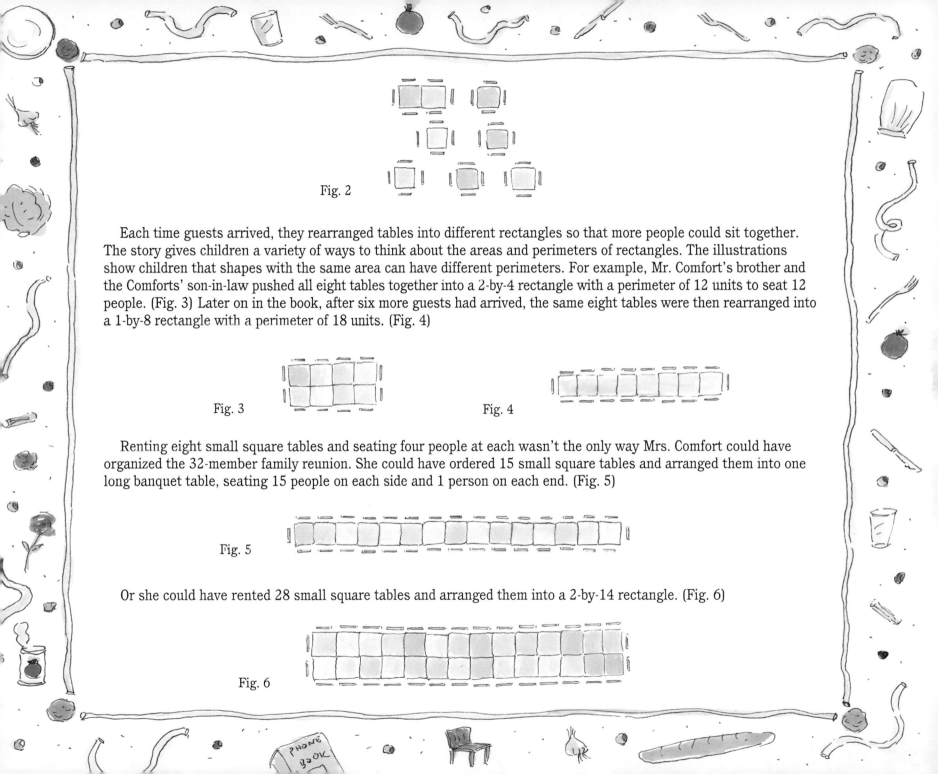

Fig. 2

Each time guests arrived, they rearranged tables into different rectangles so that more people could sit together. The story gives children a variety of ways to think about the areas and perimeters of rectangles. The illustrations show children that shapes with the same area can have different perimeters. For example, Mr. Comfort's brother and the Comforts' son-in-law pushed all eight tables together into a 2-by-4 rectangle with a perimeter of 12 units to seat 12 people. (Fig. 3) Later on in the book, after six more guests had arrived, the same eight tables were then rearranged into a 1-by-8 rectangle with a perimeter of 18 units. (Fig. 4)

Fig. 3

Fig. 4

Renting eight small square tables and seating four people at each wasn't the only way Mrs. Comfort could have organized the 32-member family reunion. She could have ordered 15 small square tables and arranged them into one long banquet table, seating 15 people on each side and 1 person on each end. (Fig. 5)

Fig. 5

Or she could have rented 28 small square tables and arranged them into a 2-by-14 rectangle. (Fig. 6)

Fig. 6

Sixteen small square tables would have worked, if they were grouped as four larger square tables, each seating eight people. (Fig. 7) Mrs. Comfort could have also used 12 small square tables arranged into four rectangles with eight seats at each. (Fig. 8)

Fig. 7

Fig. 8

In each of these examples, the perimeter of the rectangle, or the combined perimeters of several rectangles, remained constant at 32 units, making it possible to seat all 32 people. However, the area of each arrangement is different, depending upon the number of small square tables needed.

Mrs. Comfort's solution was the most economical because she rented the fewest tables needed to seat everyone. Her arrangement produced the smallest possible total table area—8 square units—while still maintaining a combined perimeter of 32 units.

Extending Children's Learning

You can help extend children's learning after reading the story, by trying any or all of the following:

1. Cut out squares of cardboard or use small square tiles so that children can construct the different ways the guests in the story arranged the tables. Help children experiment so they can see that Mrs. Comfort ordered the fewest tables possible. You may want to have them reconstruct some of the alternatives above.

2. If children are interested, go through the book again and help them draw a picture of each new table rearrangement and figure out how many people could be seated at each. Use the words area and perimeter to talk about the size of each arrangement and the number of people it seats.

3. Use the cardboard squares, tiles, or drawings to investigate the following problem: Suppose there were going to be just 12 people at the family reunion. What different table arrangements are possible? Which arrangement would use the fewest tables? Which arrangement would use the most tables? (For additional challenges, try the same problem for 16, 24, 36, or any other number of people.)

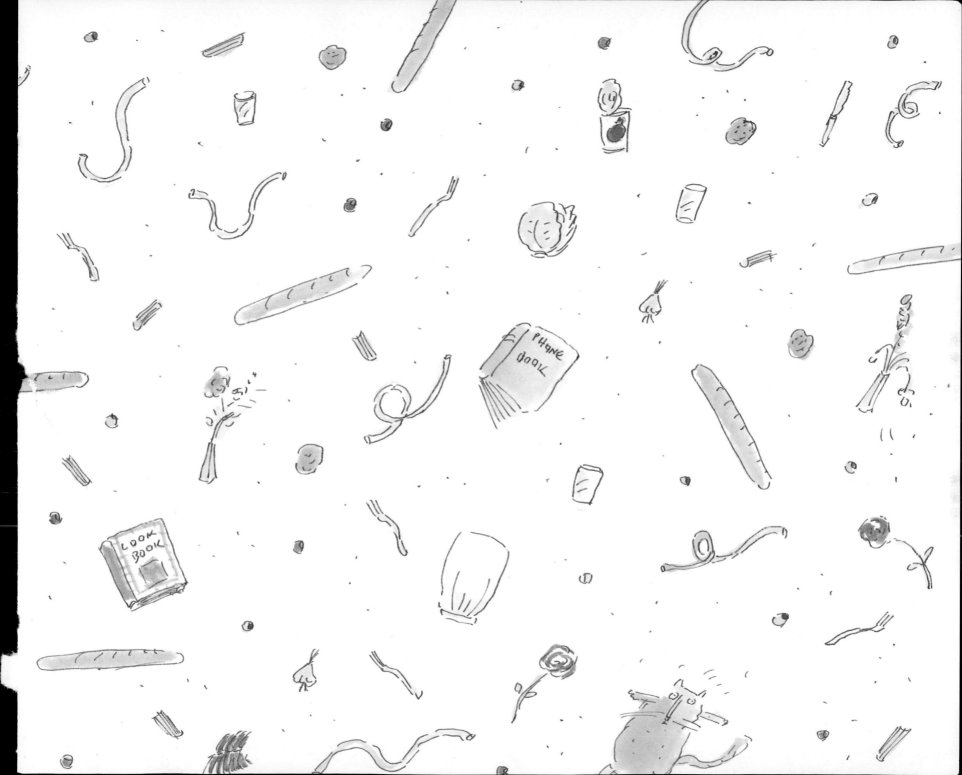

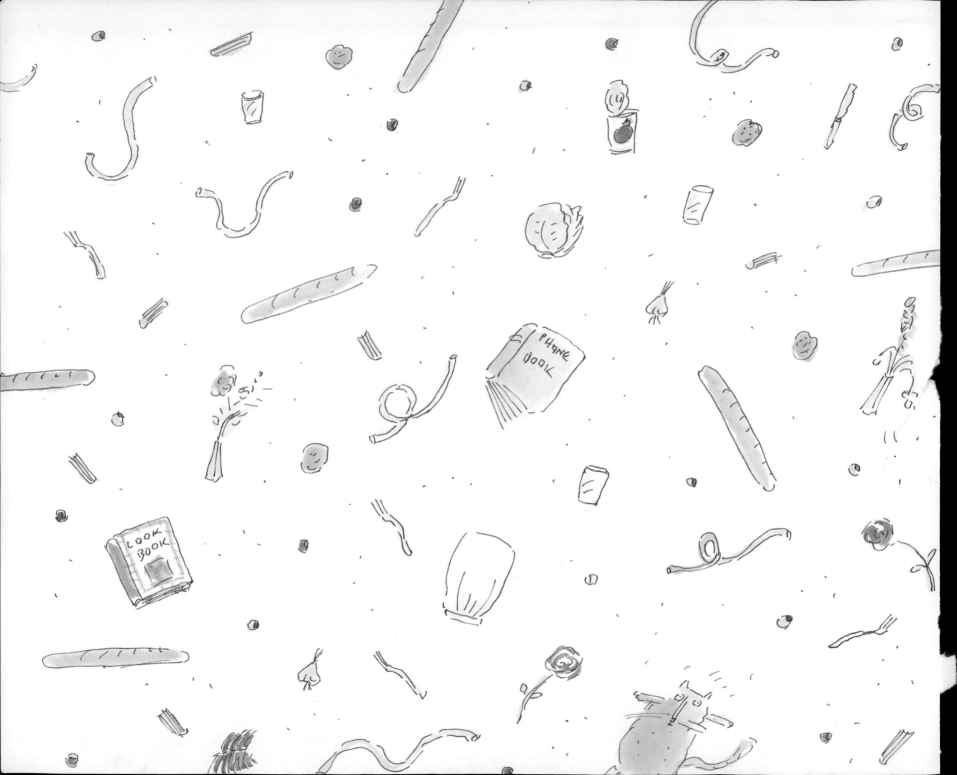